Moloka‘i

Maui

Lāna‘i

Kaho‘olawe

Hawai‘i

Ocean

Dedication

To *keiki* everywhere~

May you find joy and wonderment in these islands that I love.

~T.Y.

ISLAND HERITAGE™
P U B L I S H I N G
A DIVISION OF THE MADDEN CORPORATION

94-411 Kōʻaki Street
Waipahu, Hawaiʻi 96797-2806
Orders: (800) 468-2800
Information: (808) 564-8800
Fax: (808) 564-8877
islandheritage.com

ISBN: 1-59700-507-X
First Edition, Tenth Printing—2014
COP140910

Dear *Keiki*,
In Hawai'i we saw so many wonderful things,
we wanted to share them with you...

From Hawai'i with Aloha, Grandma and Grandpa

Exploring the Islands Together

Written and Illustrated by **Tammy Yee**

ISLAND HERITAGE™
PUBLISHING

Dear *Keiki*,

Hawai'i is the 50th state. It is far away in the middle of the Pacific Ocean. Do you see the state flag? The eight major islands—Hawai'i, Maui, Moloka'i, Lāna'i, Kaho'olawe, O'ahu, Kaua'i, and Ni'ihau—are represented by the eight stripes on the flag. Hawai'i's 124 other small islands, reefs, and shoals are home to sea birds, sea turtles, and rare Hawaiian monk seals.

Hawai'i is called the Aloha State because its people are warm and kind. They taught Grandpa and me some Hawaiian words. *Tūtū* means "grandmother." *Keiki* means "child." And aloha has many meanings like "hello," "goodbye," and "love."

From Hawai'i with aloha,
Grandma and Grandpa

Kure
Atoll

Midway
Atoll

Pearl &
Hermes Atoll

Laysan
Island

Lisianski
Island

Maro
Reef

French
Frigate
Shoals

Necker
Island

Nihoa

Kaua'i

Ni'ihau

O'ahu

Moloka'i

Lāna'i

Maui

Kaho'olawe

Hawai'i

2

Red-Footed Booby

HAWAI‘I
The Aloha State

3

Kīlauea, which means "spewing" or "much spreading," is home to Pele, the Hawaiian fire goddess. Pele has a hot temper. She once challenged the snow goddess Poliʻahu to a sled race. When Pele found herself losing, she sent rivers of lava after Poliʻahu in a fit of anger! Poliʻahu fled to Mauna Kea, covering it in a mantel of snow. From there the goddesses battled, fire against ice!

Kilauea volcano eruption.

Hawai'i Volcanoes National Park

Dear *Keiki*,

Hawai'i island is nicknamed the Big Island because it's more than twice as large as all the other major islands combined—and it's still growing! The Hawaiian Islands were made by volcanoes and some are still active. Kilauea Volcano has been erupting since 1983 and has spewed enough lava to fill more than a million Olympic-sized swimming pools! Can you see where the lava flows into the ocean? Plumes of steam shoot hundreds of feet into the sky!

From Hawai'i with aloha,
Grandma and Grandpa

Dear *Keiki*,

Who says sand must be white to be beautiful? The sand at Punaluʻu Beach is jet black and glistens in the sun!* Basking sea turtles enjoy the beach as well. Do you see two sea turtles? See how they are different? One is a *honu* (green sea turtle) and the other, with the pointed snout and jagged-edged shell, is a *honu ʻea* (hawksbill turtle). Both are endangered and nest in Hawaiʻi. We must not disturb them.

Fresh water springs flow from the mountains into Punaluʻu Bay. Long ago, Hawaiians would dive to the floor of the bay to collect this fresh water in hollowed gourds. Legend says the water was a gift from Kauila, a magical sea turtle who sometimes transformed herself into a girl so she could play with children. I wonder if one of the turtles is Kauila?

From Hawaiʻi with aloha,
Grandma and Grandpa

black sand

green sand

*Hawaiʻi is famous for its white sand beaches. However, sand on the Big Island can also be black or green because of its active volcanoes. Black sand is formed in steam explosions as hot lava enters the sea. These bits of black volcanic glass are then pulverized by waves. Green sand is made of sparkling green olivine crystals that form as lava cools.

Honu (Hawaiian green sea turtle)

Lei-draped *pā'ū* rider in a parade.

Dear *Keiki*,

Hula is more than just a dance. It has preserved Hawaiian culture for generations through ancient chants and storytelling. Missionaries arriving in Hawai'i thought hula was improper and discouraged it. King Kalākaua, the Merrie Monarch, revived the tradition of hula. In Hilo, hula is celebrated in honor of King Kalākaua at the Merrie Monarch Festival. *Hālau* (dance schools) from across the United States and from as far away as Japan come to perform!

Do you see the parade? See the hula dancers? The feathered rattles are called *'uli'ulī*. The bamboo rattles are *pū'ili*. There's even a royal court with a king and a queen! Each island is represented by a beautiful princess wearing a satin robe and riding on a horse draped in lei.

From Hawai'i with aloha,
Grandma and Grandpa

Grandma or Grandpa can help you make a paper lei (flower garland):
Materials: Thirty-inch length of string, drinking straws, construction paper, and scissors.
Instructions: Cut the straws into one-inch lengths. Cut the construction paper into flowers two inches wide. String your lei, alternating straws and paper flowers. Tie the ends and wear your lei!

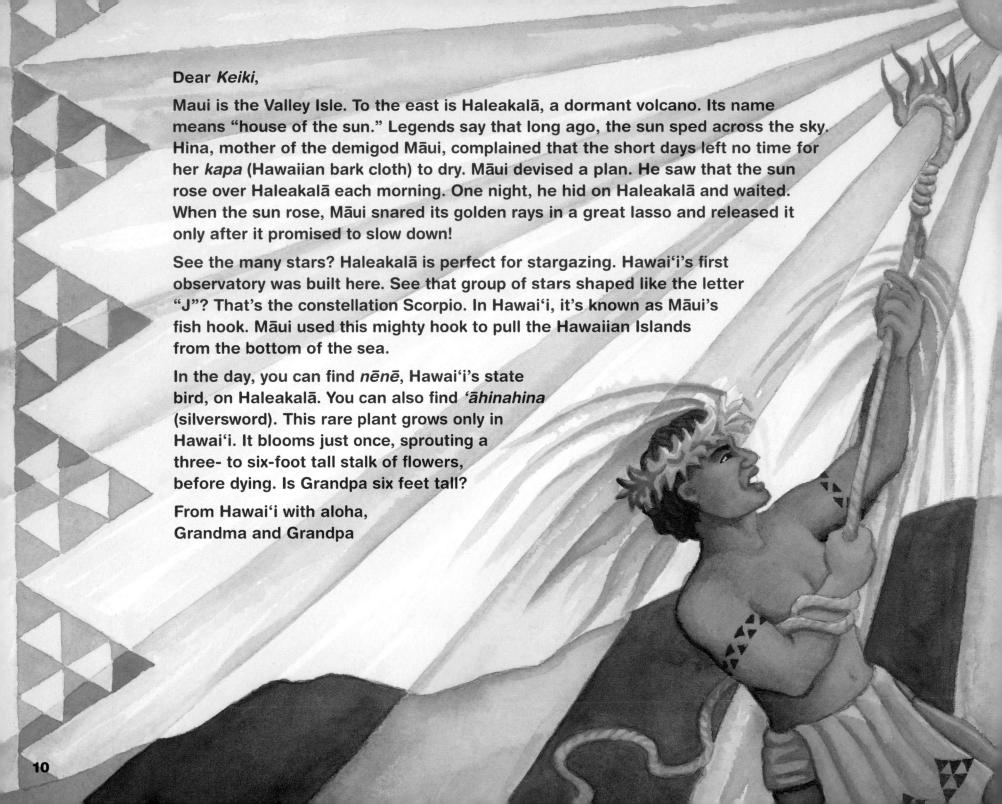

Dear *Keiki*,

Maui is the Valley Isle. To the east is Haleakalā, a dormant volcano. Its name means "house of the sun." Legends say that long ago, the sun sped across the sky. Hina, mother of the demigod Māui, complained that the short days left no time for her *kapa* (Hawaiian bark cloth) to dry. Māui devised a plan. He saw that the sun rose over Haleakalā each morning. One night, he hid on Haleakalā and waited. When the sun rose, Māui snared its golden rays in a great lasso and released it only after it promised to slow down!

See the many stars? Haleakalā is perfect for stargazing. Hawai'i's first observatory was built here. See that group of stars shaped like the letter "J"? That's the constellation Scorpio. In Hawai'i, it's known as Māui's fish hook. Māui used this mighty hook to pull the Hawaiian Islands from the bottom of the sea.

In the day, you can find *nēnē*, Hawai'i's state bird, on Haleakalā. You can also find *'āhinahina* (silversword). This rare plant grows only in Hawai'i. It blooms just once, sprouting a three- to six-foot tall stalk of flowers, before dying. Is Grandpa six feet tall?

From Hawai'i with aloha,
Grandma and Grandpa

MAUI

Haleakalā

Science City on Haleakalā

Humpback mother and calf

Lahaina

Dear *Keiki*,

Thar she blows! Hawai'i is the largest breeding ground for humpback whales. Each winter, whales swim three thousand miles from Alaska to mate and calve (give birth) in Hawaiian waters. The whales do not eat during their entire stay in Hawai'i. In May, they return to Alaska to feed on small fish and tiny shrimp-like creatures called krill.

Do you see the mother humpback whale? She's as long as a school bus (forty-five feet) and weighs as much as eight elephants (forty tons). See the black and white pattern on her tail? Each whale has a different pattern on its fluke. Scientists studying whales use these patterns like fingerprints to identify the whales. Mother whale stays close to her baby. Her newborn calf weighs as much as a car (three thousand pounds) and drinks one hundred gallons of milk a day! How much milk do you drink?

From Hawai'i with aloha,
Grandma and Grandpa

Dear *Keiki*,

Now we're on Moloka'i! Along the coast we saw a series of ancient Hawaiian fishponds—more than seventy ponds in all. A fisherman told us they were built nearly seven hundred years ago. Small fish and ocean water enter the ponds through slats in wooden gates. When the fish grow too large to swim back out, they become trapped and can easily be caught. Later, the kind fisherman shared his lunch with us. The salty, crunchy *limu* (seaweed) was *'ono* (delicious)! No wonder Moloka'i is called the Friendly Isle.

From Hawai'i with aloha,
Grandma and Grandpa

MOLOKA'I

Fishponds

Moloka'i fishpond

15

Dear *Keiki*,

Time stands still on Moloka'i. This is the birthplace of hula, where there are no traffic lights, no traffic jams, and no high rises. One-third of the island is a working ranch where *paniolo* (Hawaiian cowboys) rustle cattle much as they did one hundred years ago. Many have lived here for many generations.

Hālawa Valley is the site of Moloka'i's oldest settlements. A thousand Hawaiians may have lived here, growing taro in some seven hundred fields. Do you see the stone walls? Those are the remains of great *heiau* (temples), *lo'i* (terraced taro patches) and irrigation canals. Do you see the steep cliffs circling the valley? Moloka'i's sea cliffs are the tallest in the world—almost four thousand feet high! They guard lush rainforests and pristine valleys that are home to some of Hawai'i's most endangered plants and animals.

From Hawai'i with aloha,
Grandma and Grandpa

Moloka'i sea cliffs

Hālawa
Valley

MOLOKAʻI

17

Pu'u Pehe (Sweetheart Rock)

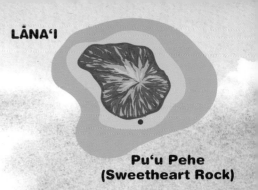

Pu'u Pehe, *or "Sweetheart Rock," is named after the beautiful daughter of a Maui chief. Hidden in a sea cave by her jealous husband, Pu'u Pehe drowned when storm waves crashed into her hideaway. Atop the eighty-foot tall rock lies a stone platform. Although legend says this is the final resting place of the beautiful maiden, it is now believed to be a shrine for bird hunters.*

Dear *Keiki*,

Lāna'i, the Pineapple Island, didn't get its name from its shape. Rather, it was once home to the world's largest pineapple plantation. Three out of four of the world's pineapples were once grown on Lāna'i!

Do you see the pineapples? Do they look like pine cones? Spanish explorers thought so, too, and that's how the pineapple got its name. Grandpa and I learned that pineapples are rich in vitamin C. Sailors brought them aboard their ships to protect them from scurvy. Do you know how to grow a pineapple? Simply cut off the top of the fruit and plant the top in soil. Make sure it has plenty of water and sunshine. Would you like to grow a pineapple? Maybe we can grow one together!

From Hawai'i with aloha,
Grandma and Grandpa

Dear *Keiki*,

O'ahu is our next stop. Three out of every four people living in Hawai'i live on this island—mostly in Honolulu, the state's capital. That's why O'ahu is nicknamed the Gathering Place. Our gathering place was at Aloha Tower, where we were greeted by hula dancers. Do you see their graceful hands? They tell stories of rainbows and swaying palms. One dancer tried to teach Grandpa the hula. Would you like to learn the hula, too?

Afterwards, we rode the elevator to the top of Aloha Tower. Built in 1926, the tower has long been a beacon for ships entering Honolulu Harbor and was once the tallest building in Hawai'i. How tall is it? Imagine standing on the head of ten giraffes—184 feet high! From the viewing deck we counted tug boats, cargo ships, and cruise ships. Where do you think all those ships came from?

**From Hawai'i with aloha,
Grandma and Grandpa**

P.S. How many aloha shirts can you find? How many lei?

Aloha Tower at night.

Dear *Keiki*,

At Hanauma Bay the water is sparkling turquoise and as clear as glass! Grandpa and I went snorkeling and played a game of who could find the most fish. We saw lemon-yellow butterflyfish, a fish with a beak like a parrot, and a shy octopus playing peek-a-boo in the coral. Can you find them too? One fish looked like it was wearing a black mask like a raccoon! It's a *humuhumunukunukuāpua'a*, Hawai'i's state fish.

We learned a lot at Hanauma Bay. We learned that corals are living animals related to jellyfish and sea anemones. Some corals grow so slowly, they would need one hundred years to grow as tall as a seven-year-old boy (about four feet). We also learned that Hanauma Bay is a flooded volcanic crater. I've never swam in a volcanic crater before—have you?

From Hawai'i with aloha,
Grandma and Grandpa

O'AHU

Hanauma Bay

Hanauma Bay

Fish Identification Card

Humuhumunukunukuāpua'a
Reef Triggerfish

Uhu
Palenose Parrotfish

Moa
Spotted Boxfish

Pāku'iku'i
Achilles Tang

'Ōmilu
Bluefin Trevally

Lauhau
Fourspot Butterflyfish

Manini
Convict Tang

Lauwiliwili
Milletseed Butterflyfish

Kihikihi
Moorish Idol

23

Dear *Keiki*,

Are there diamonds on Diamond Head? Early British sailors thought so when they found calcite crystals there—that's how Diamond Head got its name. Hawaiians call it Lē'ahi because it looks like the brow of an *'ahi* (tuna fish). Today, you can drive into the crater of this volcanic tuff cone and hike to the rim. From there you can see all of Waikīkī.

Waikīkī Beach is a playground for locals and tourists alike. Grandpa and I explored Waikīkī's ocean floor in a submarine. We saw two ships and two aircraft that were sunk off Waikīkī Beach to provide shelter for sea life. Later, we watched surfers riding waves. One man had a tiny dog that stood on his board as he surfed. Grandpa says he's seen that dog before, and he's nicknamed him Surf Puppy. He sure looks familiar—maybe we'll be seeing more of him!

From Hawai'i with aloha,
Grandma and Grandpa

calcite

Hawaiians enjoyed surfing. Men, women, and children rode on wooden boards as long as twenty-four feet. Now, people also wind surf, kite surf, and body surf. In the winter, storms at sea drive monster surf toward O'ahu's North Shore. Imagine riding waves as tall as a three-story building and more powerful than a locomotive! Only the bravest, most skillful surfers can ride these giants!

Waikiki and Diamond Head

O'AHU

Waikiki

25

'Iolani Palace

Kamehameha Day Parade marches past King Kamehameha's statue.

Dear *Keiki*,

Hawai'i is home to the only royal palace in the United States. 'Iolani Palace, built in 1882 by King Kalākaua, is in the heart of Honolulu. It had a lot of fancy upgrades for its time—indoor plumbing and Hawai'i's very first telephone! It even had electric lights years before the White House and Buckingham Palace! I especially liked the china and crystal in the State Dining Room, where author Robert Louis Stevenson was an occasional guest.

Across the street from the palace stands a statue of King Kamehameha. More than two hundred years ago, he unified the Hawaiian Islands and brought about a time of peace. On Kamehameha Day, a parade marches past 'Iolani Palace and King Kamehameha's statue is draped in fragrant lei.

From Hawai'i with aloha,
Grandma and Grandpa

27

Dear *Keiki*,

A hop and a skip, and now we're on Kaua'i! It's so green here, it's no wonder they call it the Garden Isle. Grandpa took me on a helicopter ride over Mount Wai'ale'ale. We swooped so low my heart thump-a-thump-thumped like the helicopter blades! Do you see the waterfalls? Mount Wai'ale'ale is one of the wettest spots on Earth, with rainfall of more than four hundred inches a year.

Rain on Mount Wai'ale'ale gathers in streams and rivers, scraping loose pebbles and soil as it flows to the sea. This erosion created another one of Kaua'i's natural wonders, the Waimea Canyon. When Mark Twain saw the canyon's rosy bluffs, layered cliffs and spectacular peaks, he called it the "Grand Canyon of the Pacific." At ten miles long and 3,600 feet deep, twenty-seven Waimea Canyons stretched end to end can fit into the Grand Canyon!

From Hawai'i with aloha,
Grandma and Grandpa

Waimea Canyon

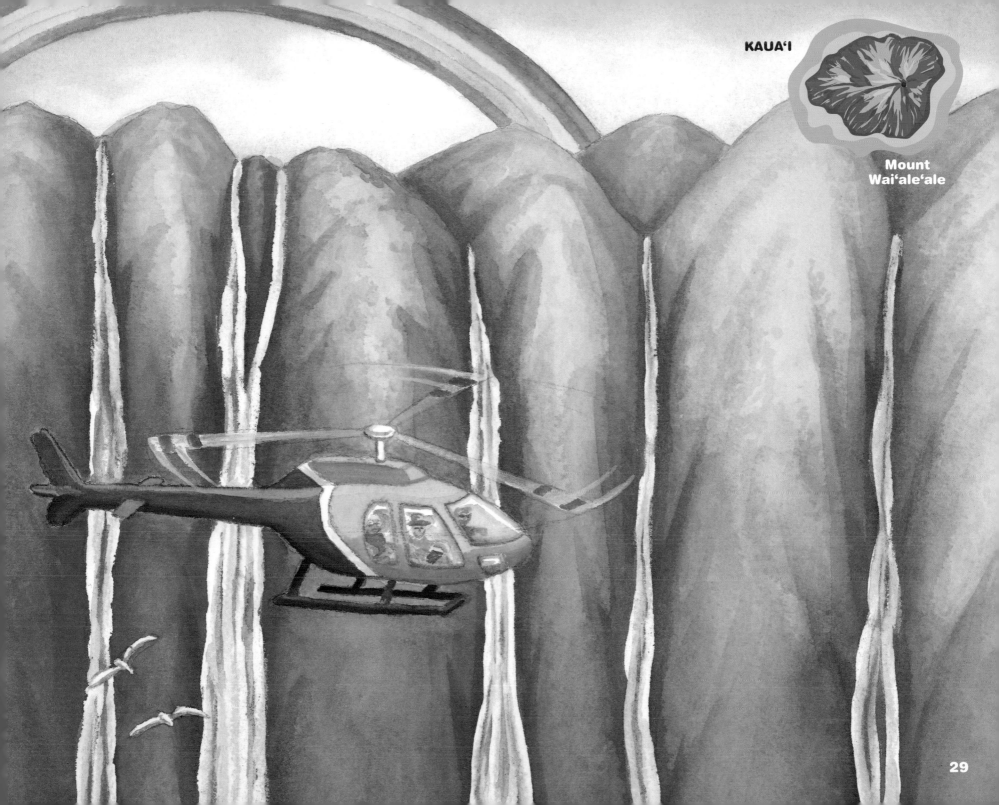

KAUAʻI

Mount
Waiʻaleʻale

29

Dear *Keiki*,

It's our final day in Hawai'i, and we celebrated with a *lū'au* (Hawaiian feast). Preparations started early this morning when Grandpa helped dig an *imu* (earthen oven) and lined it with hot stones and banana leaves. Then we lowered meat, sweet potatoes, and taro into the *imu* and covered it up. By evening our food was ready, and we ate and danced far into the night!

Before we left, we learned some important Hawaiian values: aloha (love), *ho'okipa* (hospitality), *laulima* (cooperation), *lōkahi* (unity) and *mālama* (to care for). Now we can share the spirit of Hawai'i with you!

From Hawai'i with aloha,
Grandma and Grandpa

Hawai'i, the 50th State

History: First settled by Polynesians 300-700 A.D. Hawaiian Islands unified by Kamehameha the Great in 1810. Hawaiian monarchy overthrown in 1893.

Statehood: August 21, 1959

Nickname: The Aloha State

Capital: Honolulu

Motto: *Ua mau ke ea o ka 'āina i ka pono* (The life of the land is perpetuated in righteousness.)

Anthem: *Hawai'i Pono'i*, written by King David Kalākaua

State flag: The only state flag to have flown over a kingdom, a republic, a territory and a state.

State flower: *pua ma'o hau hele*, yellow hibiscus

State fish: *humuhumunukunukuāpua'a*, Picasso triggerfish

State bird: *nēnē*, Hawaiian goose

State tree: *kukui*, candlenut

Photos from our Hawaiian adventure

Notes from Grandma and Grandpa